God's Going Too!

His Promises for Kids During Deployments

by

Cursha Pierce-Lunderman

Illustrated by Kathy Kerber

AuthorHouse™
1663 Liberty Drive, Suite 200
Bloomington, IN 47403
www.authorhouse.com
Phone: 1-800-839-8640

First published by AuthorHouse 3/31/2009

ISBN: 978-1-4389-1612-5 (sc)

Printed in the United States of America
Bloomington, Indiana

This book is printed on acid-free paper.

authorHOUSE®

For Aleyna and Sydnee,
The strongest little big girls I know. You two make being
an Army kid look fun and easy. May God continue to
bless you and keep you happy. You're such rock stars! I
love you dearly.

Our country of America is a blessed and beautiful place to live. It's a peaceful country where little boys and girls can wake up and go play outside with their friends. They can go to school and learn fun new things everyday.

But, the sad part is that America is also a country at war. Wars happen when a group of bad people from one country do something mean to people from another country. The two countries can't work things out by talking and they decide that guns and weapons will have to solve the problem. When wars happen, America calls on a group of very brave men and women in uniform to go far away and fight so everyone back at home stays safe. They are the people in the Army, Navy, Marines, and Air Force.

Joshua's dad is in the Army. He's in a special group of soldiers called the Rangers who go to war first and make it easier for the rest of the soldiers that come fight later. Joshua's scared that his dad will get hurt fighting in Iraq and he doesn't want him to go. Joshua wishes his dad could stay home and play catch with him instead of going away with the other soldiers.

But, Joshua doesn't need to be scared because wherever his dad goes, God's going too! The Bible says that God will protect Joshua's dad even though he goes to fight in scary places. God sends out angels to protect all his children in everything they do. That means angels are protecting you and your family everywhere they go too.

Evil can't get close to you harm can't get through the door. He ordered his angels to guard you wherever you go. If you stumble, they'll catch you; their job is to keep you from falling. --Psalm 91:9-12 *(The Message Bible)*

Katie's sister, Natalie, is in the Navy. She watches the weather to tell the large ships when storms and hurricanes are on the way. Natalie is about to leave on a long trip to sail the waters near Africa. Katie is worried that something might happen to her sister's boat, she wishes that Natalie could just stay home. They have so much fun baking cookies together.

But, Katie doesn't need to worry about Natalie going away because God's going too! God has power over the wind and the waves to keep Natalie's boat safe. God's word even promises that He will protect those who love him when they are in times of trouble.   Jesus protected his friends when they were in a boat a long time ago and he will do it again for your friends and family today.

Then Jesus got into the boat and started across the lake with his disciples. Suddenly, a fierce storm struck the lake, with waves breaking into the boat. But Jesus was sleeping. The disciples went and woke him up, shouting, "Lord, save us! We're going to drown!" Jesus responded, "Why are you afraid? You have so little faith!" Then he got up and rebuked the wind and waves, and suddenly there was a great calm. -- Matthew 8:23-26 (New Living Translation)

Tasha's brother, Tony, is in the Marines. Tony is on his way to fight in a place called Afghanistan. This is the third time Tony has had to go away to war and Tasha thinks something bad might happen this time. She wants Tony to just stay home and ride bikes with her instead of leaving again.

But, Tasha doesn't need to worry about Tony because God's going to Afghanistan too! The Bible says that nothing people make to hurt us will prosper. It won't be able to take us out. The bad things that might happen in life will only be a testimony, a story to tell other people of how God made everything better.

But in that coming day no weapon turned against you will succeed. You will silence every voice raised up to accuse you. These benefits are enjoyed by the servants of the Lord; their vindication will come from me. I, the Lord, have spoken!
--Isaiah 54:17 (New Living Translation)

David's mom is in the Air Force. She flies planes that take people into war and bring them back home.   David thinks her job is very scary and just wants his mom home to tuck him into bed at night. He misses her everyday.

But, David's mom will be okay because when she goes to fly planes, God's going too! He sits with her and helps her fly safely. God holds David's mom in the palm of his hand to keep her away from harm and He does the same for your loved ones too.

Because I, your God, have a firm grip on you and I'm not letting go. I'm telling you, 'Don't panic. I'm right here to help you.' --Isaiah 41:13 (The Message)

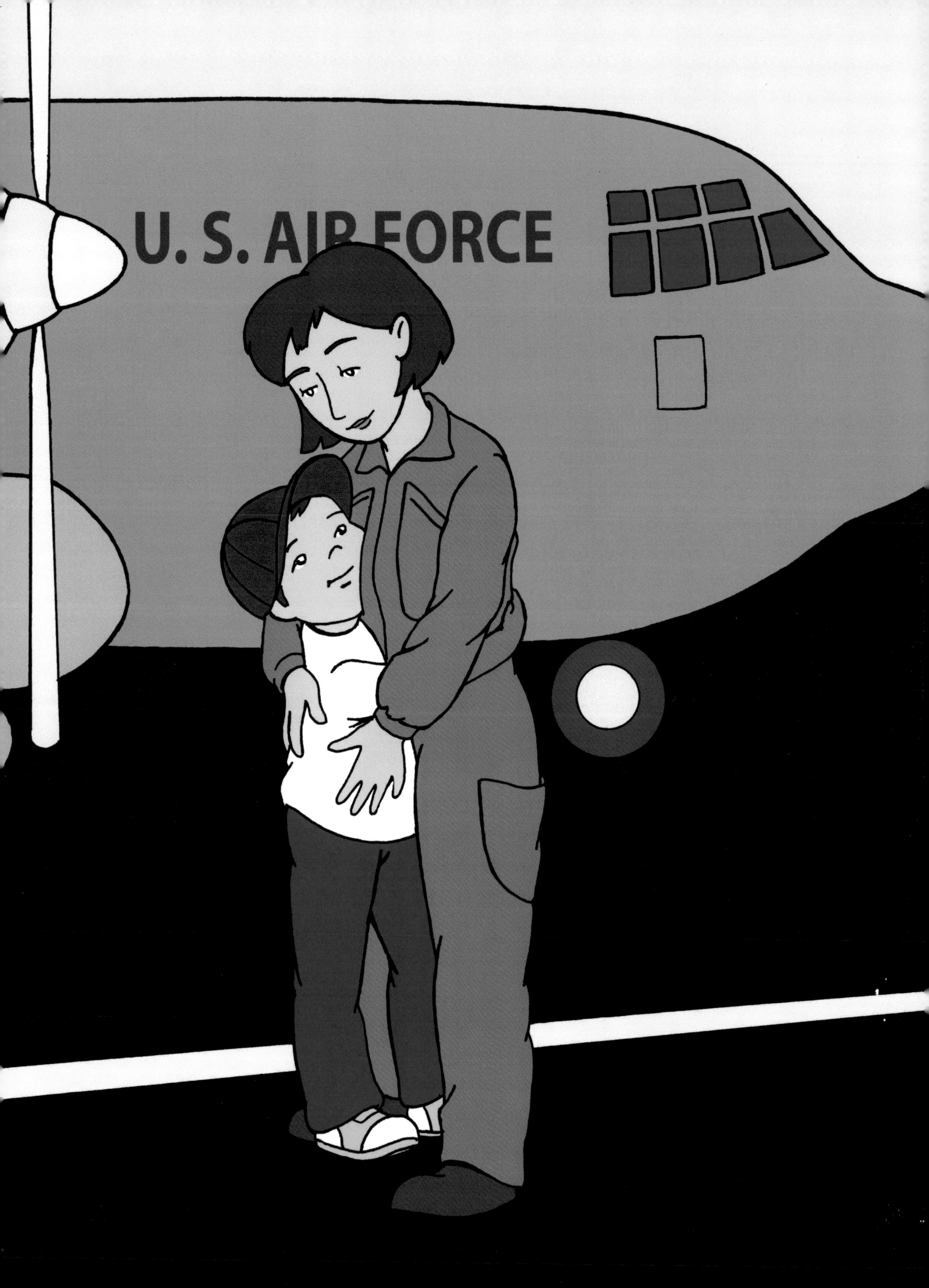
U. S. AIR FORCE

It is hard when the people you love have to go far away to fight in a war or to do their job somewhere else. But just remember that they never go alone, God always goes with them. The Bible says, *"Be strong and courageous. Do not be afraid or terrified because of them, for the Lord your God goes with you; he will never leave you nor forsake you."* --Deuteronomy 31:6 (New International Version)

When you do feel sad, scared, or alone because someone you love is far away just say a prayer for them. God is always listening to you and He loves you very much.

Let's say a prayer together:

Dear God, Please watch over my family and friends that are far away right now. Lord, please send your angels to protect them and keep them safe until they come back home. Please help me stay happy and strong while they're gone. Help me remember all of our fun times together instead of feeling sad. God, help the people in the other countries so that we can have peace and bring everyone home. In Jesus' name I pray, Amen.

About the Author

Cursha Pierce-Lunderman was raised in Fayetteville, Ga and attended Stanford University on an Army ROTC scholarship. In 2002, Cursha became a commissioned Signal Officer in the U.S. Army. As a Lieutenant, she deployed with the 25th Infantry Division, Schofield Barracks, in support of Operation Enduring Freedom in March 2004. God returned Cursha safely to the U.S. one year later and she transferred to the Army Inactive Reserves in 2006 just before giving birth to a healthy baby girl. She's now a happy Army wife, mom and author, living with her husband and two children where ever the Army sends them. Please feel free to email Cursha with any questions, comments, or cries of outrage at *cursha@serving2masters.com*. She'd love to hear from you!

CPSIA information can be obtained
at www.ICGtesting.com
Printed in the USA
239501LV00004B